EYEWITNESS TO THE
D-DAY INVASION

BY JILL ROESLER

Published by The Child's World®
1980 Lookout Drive • Mankato, MN 56003-1705
800-599-READ • www.childsworld.com

Acknowledgments
The Child's World®: Mary Berendes, Publishing Director
Red Line Editorial: Design, editorial direction, and production
Photographs ©: Bettmann/Corbis, cover, 1, 26; Everett Historical/Shutterstock
Images, 4, 15, 16; U.S. Army Signal Corps/AP Images, 7; AP Images, 9, 10, 18, 24;
Shutterstock Images, 12, 29; Sarymsakov Andrey/Shutterstock Images, 21; Farm
Security Administration/Office of War Information/Library of Congress, 22

ISBN 9781634074155

LCCN 2015946267

Printed in the United States of America
Mankato, MN
December, 2015
PA02281

ABOUT THE AUTHOR

Jill Roesler is from southern Minnesota. In addition to writing children's
books, she writes for several newspapers. Her favorite subject to research
and write about is history. In her free time, Roesler enjoys reading, traveling,
and gardening.

TABLE OF
CONTENTS

Chapter 1
PLANNING THE ATTACK 4

Chapter 2
EARLY SUCCESS 10

Chapter 3
OMAHA BEACH........................ 16

Chapter 4
MORE DANGERS 22

Chapter 5
VICTORY 26

Glossary 30
Source Notes 31
To Learn More 32
Index 32

Chapter 1

PLANNING THE ATTACK

It was the night of June 5, 1944. Darkness was falling in southern England. But thousands of **paratroopers** were awake and alert. The paratroopers were from the 101st Airborne Division of the U.S. Army. At about 10:15 p.m., they left for a very important mission.

World War II had been raging for five years. Britain, France, Canada, and the United States were all part of the Allied Powers. They were fighting against the Axis Powers. These included Germany, Italy, and Japan. In May 1940, Germany invaded France. German forces captured entire cities. Bombs devastated neighborhoods and villages. Eventually, France surrendered to Germany. The country was under German control.

The U.S. paratroopers were preparing to fly to the French region of Normandy. They would land behind enemy lines. Their mission was part of a secret attempt to **liberate** France. This plan was called Operation Overlord. The first day of the operation, June 6, would become known as D-Day. On this day, Allied forces hoped to capture French cities or towns. They also wanted to take control of roads and beaches. These locations would help them bring supplies from Britain into France.

This plan took years of preparation. Allied military leaders wanted to trick Axis leaders. They made false messages about the movements of **troops**. They even set up phony 24-hour radio broadcasts. German spies reported the false information. They believed that the Allies would attack Pas-de-Calais, France. German leaders sent many of their troops to defend this area.

The Allies really planned to attack Normandy. The Normandy region is 150 miles (241.4 km) southwest of Pas-de-Calais. By launching an unexpected attack, the Allies could catch German forces by surprise. They could capture cities in the Normandy region. Then the Allies could retake France.

For months, more than 150,000 Allied troops trained for the battle. The troops came from Britain, Canada, and the United States. Normandy was across the English Channel from their training ground. American General Dwight D. Eisenhower was leading the D-Day attack. An experienced military commander, Eisenhower knew that the plan was risky. If German leaders found out about it, they could send more soldiers to Normandy. They might defeat the Allied troops. Stormy weather could also ruin the Allies' plan. And even if the plan succeeded, many men could die. But Eisenhower also knew that D-Day could be a turning point in the war. It could help the Allies finally defeat the Axis Powers. Before the invasion, Eisenhower spoke to the troops. "The eyes of the world are upon you," he told them.[1]

Jim Martin, a U.S. Army paratrooper, understood the importance of the mission. "We knew that the success was going to hinge on us," he said. "We were absolutely certain of that. Eisenhower was too. That's why he made the decision to send us in."[2]

▲ **General Dwight D. Eisenhower spoke to Allied troops on D-Day.**

That night, the skies were cloudy. Rain poured down on the paratroopers. Many wondered if the attack would happen. But finally, they got the order to leave. Pilots and paratroopers slogged through mud to get to the planes.

Near midnight, the planes reached Normandy. Aircraft gliders dropped more than 6,600 paratroopers into northwest France. The paratroopers landed in Normandy. Many of them landed near an area with the codename Utah Beach. They did all of this in the dark. A larger attack was planned for later in the morning of June 6. The paratroopers would help the Allied forces prepare.

"The rain kept falling harder and harder. . . . We thought for sure the whole operation would be called off. Suddenly a runner poked his head through the tent opening and said, 'This is it, let's go.'"

—Donald Burgett, 101st Airborne Division of the U.S. Army[3]

Strong winds caused many paratroopers to land far from their targets. Some were killed making the jump. German soldiers shot them down with rifles. Martin's unit lost radios and other equipment. They struggled to communicate with each other. Those who survived the jump bombed bridges, railroads, and vehicles. They cut telephone lines. They wanted to prevent German forces from sending more troops to the coast. Despite some losses, the paratroopers succeeded

▲ **U.S. paratroopers prepared to fly into France.**

in their goals. Allied forces prepared for the next stage of the attack.

By early morning on June 6, the Allied troops were ready. Planes would drop bombs. Warships would bring soldiers, tanks, and other equipment. The soldiers would land on the beaches of Normandy. In that first day, they hoped to get past German defenses on the beaches. Then they would secure land near ports and roads. This would help them continue to make gains in France.

Chapter 2

EARLY SUCCESS

Hours after the paratroopers landed, Allied ships approached the beaches. Allied bomber planes soared overhead. The ships were loaded with troops, tanks, and equipment. U.S. troops landed on Utah Beach and Omaha Beach in the west. British and Canadian troops landed on the other three beaches, in the east: Gold Beach, Sword Beach, and Juno Beach.

At sunrise, warplanes began to drop bombs on German targets. By 6:00 a.m., nearly 450 Allied bomber planes swarmed above the coast. They released 1,200 tons of bombs on the Germans down below. Werner Kortenhaus, a German soldier, remembered the startling sight. "The noise was enormous, the sight awesome," he said.[4]

At 7:00 a.m., British warships faced rough, choppy seas on Gold Beach. Troops had to exit the ships several yards from the coast. They waded through the water to the shore. Heavy supplies, including jackets and weapons, weighed them down.

Crowds of British soldiers struggled to reach the shore. But the Allies' trick had worked. The German military was not expecting them. Top German military leaders were far from Normandy. Only smaller divisions of German soldiers were left to respond to the attack. These soldiers fought hard, but they were outnumbered. Many were also inexperienced. German leaders had sent more skilled soldiers to Pas-de-Calais.

The British soldiers unloaded special tanks from the ships. The tanks, known as "funnies," removed **land mines** from the area. They helped the soldiers march safely on the flat, sandy beach.

▲ **British military units used tanks to remove land mines.**

Soldiers met few German troops or natural obstacles. Within one hour of landing, they had advanced beyond the beach.

Meanwhile, other British warships landed on Sword Beach. Soldiers waded to the coast under gunfire from German forces. Injured British troops struggled to make it to shore. But the German forces were outnumbered. Funnies helped British soldiers clear mines. The soldiers reached the beach exits quickly. They headed toward the French city of Caen.

On Juno Beach, the 3rd Canadian Infantry Division had a rougher start. Stormy weather delayed the division's landing. When the soldiers landed, they faced heavy gunfire from German forces. Bullets zipped past the Canadian soldiers, but they kept fighting.

Cliff Chadderton was an officer of the Royal Winnipeg Rifles. Many troops in his **regiment** were well trained. But they had never seen battle before. "They found the strength to carry on," Chadderton said. "By six o'clock on the evening of D-Day, the Winnipegs had gone further **inland** than most of the planners thought possible."[5] There were 14,000 Canadian soldiers on the beach. When the battle was over, the division had lost only 340 men. The soldiers marched farther into France.

American troops at Utah Beach were lucky. Strong ocean currents stopped the ships from reaching their planned landing

"I was surprised it hadn't been worse than it was. I was pleased I was in one piece. . . . it had been a lot easier than what I expected."

—*Russell King, British sergeant major at Sword Beach*[6]

spot. They had to choose a new location. But the new landing spot was better. The troops were able to reach land more easily. They came under fire from German soldiers but suffered few **casualties**. A total of 21,000 U.S. soldiers fought on that beach. Only 197 were killed or injured. Once they cleared the beach, the troops headed inland. Their goal was to capture land at Cherbourg. This was a port that would help the Allies receive supplies in France.

Attacks at four of the five beaches had gone smoothly. By midmorning, Allied troops had arrived at the four beaches. Some had even made it past the beaches. But the battle on Omaha Beach proved more difficult—and deadly.

American troops waded to the shore at Utah Beach. ▶

Chapter 3

OMAHA BEACH

At 6:36 a.m., the first group of U.S. boats reached the Omaha Beach shoreline. Troops jumped from the boats. They began wading through waist-deep water. But German troops were waiting for them. "It seemed like the whole world exploded," said U.S. Lieutenant Robert Edlin.[7] Machine guns rattled. Gun shots caused men to topple into the water. Others had to step over them to reach the shore.

Finally, American soldiers began to reach land. The men stepped onto the sand. Then they noticed something strange. The beach was almost completely silent.

"All the gunfire had lifted," Edlin said. "The sun was just coming up over the coast. I saw a bird . . . fly across the front of the boat, just like life was going on as normal."[8]

The silence did not last long. The troops on Omaha Beach had walked into a trap. Suddenly, hundreds of German troops began firing their rifles. One deadly machine gun could shoot 1,500 bullets every minute. Bullets rained down on the American soldiers. They suffered heavy casualties. Within 10 minutes, the first wave of soldiers was almost completely wiped out.

"The beach sounded like a beehive with the bullets flying around," said Captain Joseph T. Dawson.

"There came something like a peppering of hail, heavy hail. . . . I realized it was enemy machine-gun fire."

—*Lieutenant Robert Edlin*[9]

▲ **Field Marshal Erwin Rommel (front right) commanded the German forces on the coast of France.**

"You could hear them hit and you could hear them pass through the air."[10]

Erwin Rommel was in charge of the German forces at Normandy. He was known as a powerful leader. Rommel was a weapons expert who often used bold ideas. He had constructed 2,400 miles (3,862 km) of **bunkers** and other defenses along the French coast. This line of bunkers was called the Atlantic Wall.

There were eight bunkers on Omaha Beach. When the Americans landed, many German soldiers waited in these shelters. The concrete shelters kept German soldiers safe from attack. Steel posts inside the bunkers made them almost impossible to destroy. The bunkers had machine guns. But gunfire was not the only problem the Allied soldiers faced. Another danger was lurking in the sand.

Rommel had set up traps on Omaha Beach. One area was nicknamed the "Devil's Garden." It contained thousands of wooden stakes. An explosive mine was attached to each stake. There were 34,827 stakes on Omaha Beach alone. The stakes were 10 feet (3 m) tall. Nearby soldiers could spot them in the sand. But at high tide, the water would hide the stakes.

Omar Bradley was the American commander of the attack on Omaha Beach. He had heard of the Devil's Garden. Bradley knew that American troops should land when the tide was low. They would be safer from the mine-capped stakes. But they faced other dangers. During low tide, enemy soldiers could see them more clearly. When the Allied soldiers landed, German forces were waiting for them.

Soldiers at Omaha Beach arrived in waves, or groups. The first group was supposed to be past the beach by the time the second group arrived. But heavy gunfire and Rommel's traps delayed them. At 8:00 a.m., soldiers in the first wave were still on the beach.

Other waves of soldiers were arriving. The crowding made movement difficult. And German soldiers could easily shoot into the crowds.

The Atlantic Wall included bunkers with powerful weapons. ▶

Chapter 4

MORE DANGERS

By midmorning, most of the D-Day units had made progress. On every beach except Omaha, troops had begun to reach the exits. British and American news stations began reporting on the invasion.

On Omaha Beach, all of the warships had arrived. But not all of the Allied men made it safely to land. Machine-gun fire kept blaring. Many men

◄ **As people heard about the D-Day invasion, they held rallies to support the troops.**

were hit while they were still several yards away from the beach. Others ducked behind obstacles on the beach. Some sprinted through the Devil's Garden. "There was a large German bunker in front of us," said Captain Edward McGregor. "Its machine-gun fire hit us every time we tried to move."[11]

Slowly, the American soldiers advanced. But once soldiers made it past the beach, they faced other challenges. First, they had to pass through a large barbed-wire fence. Sergeant Harley Reynolds ran for the fence. "I was the first one through the wire from my boat," said Reynolds. "You could hear the bullets zipping by."[12] Reynolds kept his head down as he ran. The bullets were breaking up bits of rock all around him. These rock pieces hit him in the face.

Once through the barbed wire, soldiers came up against tall cliffs. Approximately 90 feet (27 m) tall, the cliffs wouldn't be easy to scale. To make matters worse, soldiers carried packs of supplies. These packs weighed from 60 to 90 pounds (27 to 41 kg). Soldiers struggled over the cliffs, lugging their heavy packs to safety.

There were five paths through the cliffs. But four of the five paths were dirt roads. Only one was paved. On the dirt roads, the already exhausted soldiers struggled through mud and puddles. These obstacles slowed their progress.

Rommel's troops had also placed 40,000 hidden land mines around the cliffs. These mines were especially deadly. Normal mines **detonate** on the ground. They hit only the soldiers who step on them. But Rommel created mines that could hit several

▲ **American troops took shelter from enemy fire on D-Day.**

men at once. The mines did not detonate on the ground. Instead, they flew into the air and exploded. The mines released pieces of metal that hit and injured nearby troops.

Despite these injuries, the troops moved forward. At 2:00 p.m., they reached the small city of Vierville. Capturing small cities was an important step in liberating France. After hours of fighting, American troops gained a small **foothold** in the area. The situation was still dangerous. But the troops could expand on this foothold. It could help them win more victories.

Meanwhile, the troops from Sword Beach marched toward Caen. Capturing this city was an important D-Day goal. It would get the Allies closer to Paris, France's capital. Yet troops faced a tough 9-mile (14-km) journey from the shore. In the afternoon, they met tanks from Germany's 21st Panzer Division. Soldiers struggled to ward off the German attack.

Bomber planes swooped overhead, firing on the German forces. Nearby, French citizens tried to take shelter from the battle. One woman was preparing a meal when the troops began to pass. By the time they had left, the food was "black with dust and full of shards of glass."[13]

The troops failed to capture Caen on D-Day. But they did hold off the German attack. In the next several days, they would continue to travel inland.

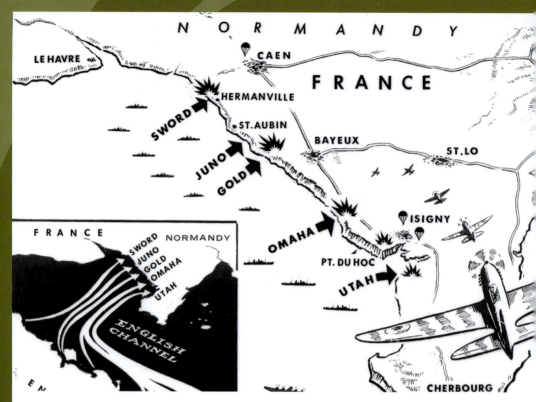

Chapter 5

VICTORY

By the end of the day on June 6, 150,000 Allied soldiers had landed in France. They had broken through German defenses on the beaches. Most units were several miles inland. General Eisenhower celebrated the troops' success. "You are truly a great allied team," he wrote in a message to all forces.[14]

Despite these gains, the Allies suffered many losses. A total of 4,413 soldiers were killed.

◀ **This map shows where Allied troops moved in on D-Day.**

Many of the survivors remembered the deaths of their comrades. "We were told not to stop and help any of our buddies," said Wilfred Bennett. He was a member of the Royal Winnipeg Rifles. "We were to carry on as best we could to get across the beach."[15]

D-Day was only the first day of a much longer series of battles. But it had truly taken German forces by surprise. By the end of June 1944, the Allies had taken control of most of Normandy. As Operation Overlord continued, Allied troops needed more weapons. They also required new vehicles. These supplies were sent from England. Delivery ships used Normandy as a port. Soon, the roads of Normandy bustled with Allied vehicles.

The 4,413 Allied soldiers who died on D-Day are still on that beach. German soldiers buried each soldier who died that day. All of the fallen D-Day troops are buried on a bluff near

"Sometimes I wondered if the battles would ever end. We seemed to be fighting all day, every day. We couldn't see an end to it."

—*Peter Davies, a British soldier*[16]

> "I am sure that the trees and the fields on the evening before D-Day were really green. Twenty-four hours later they had lost their freshness and were coated with the dust which D-Day had raised."
>
> —*Alan Melville, a British war reporter*[17]

Omaha Beach. There are 9,387 people buried in the Normandy American Cemetery. A white cross marks each grave.

For weeks, the Allied troops continued to march through France. On August 25, 1944, the troops liberated the city of Paris. It was a major loss for the Axis Powers.

A museum in Normandy honors the soldiers ▶ who fought on D-Day.

MUSEE MEMORIAL 1944

GLOSSARY

bunkers (BUHNG-kerz): Bunkers are sturdy shelters often used during wartime. Bunkers kept soldiers safe from gunfire.

casualties (KAZH-oo-ul-teez): Casualties are people who are wounded, dead, or missing. There were many casualties on D-Day.

detonate (DET-un-ayt): To detonate is to explode. Soldiers saw bombs detonate around them.

foothold (FOOT-hohld): A foothold is a safe or secure place. After the Allies had a foothold in Normandy, they could capture other parts of France.

inland (IN-lund): When people move inland, they move away from the coast. Troops on D-Day wanted to move inland from the beaches.

land mines (LAND MAHYNZ): Land mines are explosive objects under the surface of the ground. Rommel's troops placed land mines on the beach.

liberate (LI-bur-ayt): To liberate is to set free. The Allied Powers wanted to liberate France from German control.

paratroopers (PAR-uh-troo-perz): Paratroopers are soldiers trained to parachute from an airplane. Paratroopers landed in Normandy at midnight.

regiment (REJ-i-ment): A regiment is a group of soldiers led by a colonel. Each regiment was assigned to a particular area.

troops (TROOPS): Troops are soldiers or military officers. Thousands of troops invaded Normandy on D-Day.

SOURCE NOTES

1. "Messages from Dwight D. Eisenhower." *American Merchant Marine at Normandy June 1944*. American Merchant Marine at War, 2 June 2004. Web. 24 May 2015.

2. Lisa Ferdinando. "D-Day Paratrooper Remembers Historic Jump Ahead of 70th Anniversary." *www.army.mil*. U.S. Army, 2 June 2014. Web. 24 May 2015.

3. Jon E. Lewis, ed. *Voices from D-Day: Eyewitness Accounts from the Battle for Normandy*. New York: MFJ Books, 2014. Print. 50.

4. Ibid. 99.

5. "Winnipeg Rifles." *Juno Beach: The Canadians on D-Day*. D. W. Lane, December 2014. Web. 24 May 2015.

6. Roderick Bailey. *Forgotten Voices of D-Day*. New York: Random House, 2010. Print. 369.

7-8. Jon E. Lewis, ed. 109.

9. Ibid. 100.

10. Ibid. 111.

11. Ibid. 116.

12. "D-Day 360." *Stories of Service*. PBS, 27 May 2014. Web. 20 May 2015.

13. "Invasion of Normandy, June 6, 1944: A Civilian's View." *Eyewitness to History*. Ibis Communications, 2010. Web. 20 May 2015.

14. "Messages from Dwight D. Eisenhower." 2 June 2004.

15. "D-Day, June 6, 1944." *The National World War II Museum, New Orleans*. National WWII Museum, n.d. Web. 20 May 2015.

16. Jon E. Lewis, ed. 175.

17. Ibid. 229.

TO LEARN MORE

Books

Atkinson, Rick. *D-Day: The Invasion of Normandy, 1944.* New York: Square Fish, 2015.

Demuth, Patricia Brennan, David Grayson Kenyon, and Scott Anderson. *What Was D-Day?* New York: Grosset & Dunlap, 2015.

Murray, Doug, and Anthony Williams. *D-Day: The Liberation of Europe Begins.* New York: Rosen, 2007.

Web Sites

Visit our Web site for links about the D-Day invasion:

childsworld.com/links

Note to Parents, Teachers, and Librarians: We routinely verify our Web links to make sure they are safe and active sites. So encourage your readers to check them out!

INDEX

bunkers, 19–20, 23

Caen, 12, 25

casualties on D-Day, 14, 17, 26, 27, 28

Devil's Garden, 19, 23

Eisenhower, Dwight D., 6, 7, 26

Gold Beach, 10, 11

Juno Beach, 10, 13

land mines, 11, 12, 24

Omaha Beach, 10, 14, 16–20, 22, 28

Operation Overlord, 5, 27

paratroopers, 4–9, 10

Pas-de-Calais, 5, 6, 11

Rommel, Erwin, 18–20, 24–25

Royal Winnipeg Rifles, 13, 27

Sword Beach, 10, 12, 13, 25

Utah Beach, 8, 10, 13–14